STIMULATING YOUR PROFESSIONAL CREATIVITY

Get out of your rut and unlock your creative potential

Written by Chantal Rens

Translated by Carly Probert

HOW TO SPARK YOUR PROFESSIONAL CREATIVITY

- **Problem:** How can I develop my creative talents in order to stand out in the office?
- **Uses:** Awakening your imagination allows you to think of innovative solutions to any situation – what a way to become an asset to your company!
- **Professional context:** Personal development, innovation, professional efficiency and problem-solving.
- **FAQs:**
  - Are we all creative?
  - Is creativity a recognised skill in business?
  - There is already a creative hub in my company; do I still need to develop my own creativity?
  - How can I concretely develop a creative state of mind?
  - What is the difference between imagination, creativity, invention and innovation?

Of course, being creative is a true asset, especially in a professional context of constant change and intense competition, where everything is measured increasingly in the short-term. Start-up bosses know this well: "In today's world, straight lines are rare", says Michael Brecht, founder of Doodle AG (online planning service). "You should know how to adapt your business model based on opportunities and motivate all your employees".

Do you want to shine in a meeting with your original, yet realistic ideas, but think that creativity is a gift reserved for a privileged few? Think again!

Inventiveness remains accessible, but proposing innovative solutions is something that definitely cannot be improvised. It requires work and discipline: you must establish a framework, rely on stimulation techniques, sort the crazy ideas from those that are adapted to the problem, etc. Are you still sceptical? Do you still think that this is a power reserved for marketing teams, advertising pros or new technology virtuosos? This is not the case. In many cases, you will hit the bull's eye if you dare to think outside the box and try looking at the situation with fresh eyes. Creativity can come into play through the search for new customers, developing new product packaging, organising an evening event, writing a speech, implement a revolutionary concept or managing conflict between employees.

Whether practicing solo or in a collective brainstorming session, your innovation potential can make a difference. Still, it is necessary to learn its principles. In just 50 minutes, this book will present to you the process of imagination and the tools that can help you to develop your creativity every day.

PROFESSIONAL CREATIVITY: THE BASICS

UNDERSTANDING CREATIVITY

Creative intelligence

According to Robert Sternberg (American psychologist, born in 1949), "Creativity is the ability to produce work that is: innovative (i.e. original, unexpected), good quality and appropriate (i.e. useful and respects constraints)" (Sternberg, Kaufman, & Pretz, 2002: 1). This specialist also analyses the role of intelligence in the creative process and identifies the following trio:

- **Analytical intelligence** (left hemisphere) is the ability to analyse, evaluate and solve a problem. This is academic intelligence that can be measured by IQ.
- **Practical intelligence** (right hemisphere) defines responsiveness to circumstances.
- **Creative intelligence** is the ability to invent ideas to face new and unusual situations based on experience and by soliciting imagination and intuition.

American psychologist J. P. Guilford (1897-1987) also articulates these two concepts by identifying two stages in the creative process:

- **Divergent thinking.** This is a mental process used to produce as many ideas as possible using imagination and intuition.

- **Convergent thinking.** Starting with the initial reflections, this provides an organised and operational response using a person's reasoning abilities.

Creativity is used for divergent thinking, while intelligence is more to do with convergent thinking. The two are related; there is no intelligence without creativity, and vice versa.

The creative process

In the twenties, Graham Wallas (Professor of Political Science, 1858-1932), who was very interested in psychology, distinguished four stages in the creative process:

- **Preparation.** During this time, the foundation work is carried out, which can be rather laborious, in which you define the problem and collect the information needed to solve the problem;
- **Incubation.** During this second phase, whether short or long, the brain works unconsciously by associating ideas

on the subject;

- **Enlightenment.** This is the phase when ideas emerge, where you indulge in spontaneity freely and without judgement;
- **The checking process.** This last phase involves the selection of ideas, according to the relevance and feasibility.

Different creative logics

Creativity can take many forms. Depending on your mode of operation, choose one or the other method:

- **Associative logic** is based on the free association of ideas. This is to spontaneously express as much as possible, without censorship, and smoothly linking them together. This practice is particularly useful when brainstorming;
- **Analogical logic** based on the comparison between close areas, in order to draw similarities and differences. Synectics, an American method developed by William Gordon (1919-2003) and George Prince (1918-2009), uses this approach by seeking ideas in areas that have already been explored. For example, the plan was invented by making an analogy with the bird;
- **Dreamlike logic.** Robert Desoille (French engineer and psychologist, 1890-1966) developed a method based on this logic, called "guided imagery" (RED). The person gets into a relaxed state and then imagines a particular scenario. This technique aims to reach the unconscious, in order to foster imagination;
- **Projective logic** provides original ideas by putting oneself in the shoes of characters, animals, professionals, etc. Role plays are good examples of this.

OVERCOMING OBSTACLES

Limited beliefs

For creative ideas to flow freely, we must overcome obstacles and release inhibitions that impede any innovative approach. These can be emotional: fear of being wrong, losing credibility, looking silly, being labelled as stupid, being in the minority, facing the stare of others, fear of the unknown, etc. They can also be based on cultural beliefs that hold back the potential to advance: thinking that imagination is for children, that your ideas will never be accepted in your company, needing to be right the first time without fumbling, etc.

These limiting beliefs are present daily in your unconscious. However, they are an interpretation of reality, and not a truth. To be creative, you have to escape the mould in which each individual is trapped. We must change our way of thinking and question what is thought to be possible and impossible, our experiences, our way of thinking, education, etc. We should not take knowledge for granted, but constantly try to change the way we see things. Reflecting will open new doors and develop your creativity.

Perfectionism

Everyone becomes creative and original when they are stretched beyond their obligations, restrictive rules and expectations. Therefore, accept imperfection, because it often bears the uniqueness of a concept or idea. For all those who endlessly search for their last finding before presenting it: "The best is the enemy of the good". In other words, by wanting to continually improve things, we risk spoiling what we have.

> "At the start of my career, I lost a lot of time collecting documents and taking testimonies. It seemed essential to accumulate all this material to work around the question before writing a single line. At the same time, I had to write in a hurry, so you can imagine the stress... I gradually realised that these excessive preliminary steps came at the expense of taking a fresh look at the story. Now I start directly, trusting my analytical mind and my intuition. That way, I find the most interesting and unexpected angles." – Paul R., journalist for a local newspaper

Lack of self-confidence

"I'm terrible", "I've never had imagination", "I'll lose face", "Others are smarter than me", etc. Does a true 'inner jury' of critics assail you and do you feel incessant doubts as soon as you embark on something? It is time to banish that negative voice that holds you back in your creative process and, more generally, in your fulfilment.

Start by replacing these thoughts with positive affirmations, practising the Coué method. Developed by Emile Coue (French psychologist, 1857-1926), it is used as a method of auto-suggestion for reprogramming the brain. Repeat to yourself that you will get there, you have imagination, etc.: this will help you to believe in your creative potential. Another technique is that of creative visualisation. The aim is to imagine situations in which you are full of confidence.

Sit back comfortably and close your eyes, breathe slowly and visualise yourself making a successful presentation, creating an innovative new project or comfortably presenting a lecture to 200 people. Gradually, this imaginary trust will influence your life, as long as you carry out this exercise with conviction.

TECHNIQUES TO DEVELOP YOUR CREATIVITY

Practice mental gymnastics

Creativity is primarily a state of mind to grow every day, similar to a body that we want to make strong. Systematic inquiry and the art of surprise are the basic exercises for a creative mind.

"I keep my imagination well-oiled by breaking daily routines: I change my route to work or decorate the walls of my office with new photos. But, curiosity also proves to be a powerful engine. I regularly stroll through the bookstore and leaf through magazines that are far from my natural interests or watch movies that have nothing to do with my world. Ideas can appear at any time. For example, when driving my car I found the basic concept of an advertising campaign, looking at a random poster of a competitor.

However, inspiration is not enough, ideas are what work. It takes a lot of concentration and tenacity to reach a satisfactory solution. Moreover, questioning is necessary, you have to forget about susceptibility when a project is rejected and set out on a new path with skill and enthusiasm. Experience has taught me to turn them into games and forces me to have fun." – Grégoire, creative director at advertising agency *La Chose.*

Ask yourself the following questions to analyse what creative method works for you:

- Do ideas come to you when you are alone or when exchanging with others?
- Do you prefer a zen and calm atmosphere where you are safe in your bubble (such as your office or bedroom), or are you stimulated by an active environment (jogging, housework, gardening, etc.)?
- Do you need an adrenaline boost of stress at the last minute to get the best out of yourself or do you prefer organised and marked progress over time?
- Do you have any particular habits that contribute to boosting your creativity (filing your papers first, establishing a schedule for the day, taking a stroll for a few minutes, listening to music, etc.)?

Once you have found your preferred method, make conscious use of it: this will be a sure way of getting results. For those who need a little help, there are a few easy and fun exercises detailed later that will help you to stretch your mind.

'Bissociation' or forced association

This exercise involves taking a random word from a dictionary or any paper you have at hand, and start your thinking from there. You can also choose several and try to invent a new concept in relation to these words. For example, what would you do with "light" and "pencil"? Or "shoe" and "book"? Nothing comes to mind? Think a little more and let your imagination run wild. The goal is not to create a realistic object. On the contrary, the more zany ideas, the better.

The catastrophic scenario

This exercise involves identifying what is the worst that could happen. So, ask yourself questions, such as: What will definitely make me miss my presentation? How can I make the public hate my product? What will ensure that I fail in achieving my goal? This activity may seem strange at first, but by exposing the negative, you can turn them into positives. This type of reflection is a source of creativity, not to mention fun.

The six hats

This method, developed by the Maltese psychologist Edward de Bono (born in 1933), involves adopting different viewpoints by wearing six hats of different colours in turn, each representing a way of thinking. This technique can be used both in a group and alone.

The six hat method by Edward de Bono

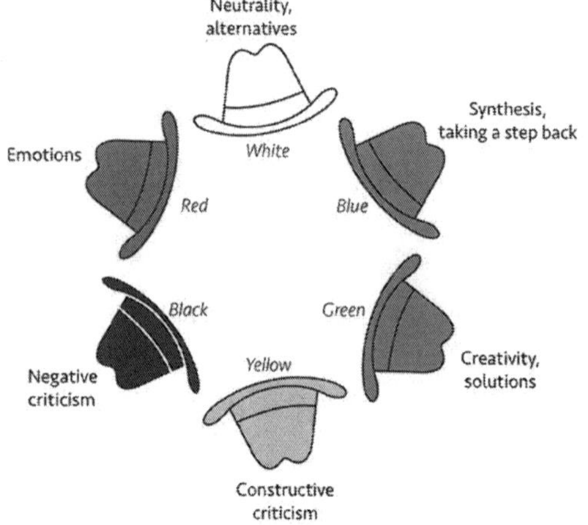

LATERAL THINKING

Edward de Bono has also theorised on lateral thinking. He fosters imagination and intuition and opposes vertical thinking that feeds on logic and realism. Moreover, he does not reject any ideas and leaves room for those that are impossible to achieve, considering this to be a step in the search for innovative solutions. This way of thinking allows you to escape from conventional thinking patterns, to change the perception of your environment and stimulate creativity. This is also called "thinking outside the box", because it tends to resolve a situation or a problem from an original and unexpected perspective. To develop lateral thinking, de Bono suggests using "sting operations", such as the six hats method, bissociation, exaggeration of the problem, distortion of the facts, misuse of an object or utopia.

Mind mapping

Developed by Tony Buzan (English psychologist, born in 1942), mind mapping is a visual representation of the thought process and therefore the links between each idea. The principle is very simple: begin with the basis of your reflection at the centre of a white sheet of paper in the form of words or drawings, then add the resulting ideas by connecting them with branches. You can use different colours to differentiate the ramifications. This view allows the brain to facilitate connections and therefore promotes the creation of ideas.

INTERACTING TO BOOST CREATIVITY

Although creativity is an individual skill, it can be boosted by teamwork. Indeed, what better way to develop new ideas than to compare them with those of your employees? Since there are almost as many different views as people, do not hesitate to enrich yourself with the points of view of others. In addition, collective creativity techniques often result in synergies that can be illustrated by the maxim of Aristotle (Greek philosopher, 384-322 B.C.): "The whole is greater than the sum of its parts". However, for this to work, it should follow the basic rules of each method.

Brainstorming

The general principles of the "brainstorming" technique, developed by Alex Osborn (American advertiser, 1888-1966), are: prohibiting any judgement or criticism, allowing the imagination to run wild, bouncing off the ideas of others to end up with a large number of ideas. During this first phase, it does not matter if these ideas are feasible or not. This analysis will come in the second phase, that of selection.

To build on this method, give your imagination free rein: the more far-fetched the idea, the better. It is easier to reel an idea in than to embellish one. Thus, exploit them shamelessly, even if you turn the other way in the end. Furthermore, you agree to pool your ideas and not succumb to competitiveness: they belong to the group and each member owns them equally. And finally, with the help of the team, identify those that can perhaps be refined to produce a new product, service or innovation.

ADVICE

Brainstorming can only work if individuals participate without fear of being judged or evaluated by others. Moreover, in order for the ideas to be as varied as possible, it is generally a good idea to bring together people from different services.

Workshop

A workshop is an exchange on a topic that has been defined in advance. It can take place on one or more days and brings together specialists who interact with a limited number of participants. Taking part in such events can help you learn new skills or develop your current skills. Do not hesitate to get some information and, if you have a choice, do not necessarily go to a workshop where the topic relates to your industry; instead, you could attempt to discover unknown areas. Friendly and collaborative, these workshops are an opportunity to develop your curiosity and creativity.

Finally, do not hesitate to discuss your ideas and test them on your colleagues around the coffee machine, over drinks after work or during your lunch break: their views might enlighten you. However, be careful that the working group does not release individual work. Clearly, collective stimulation is only there to complete your personal approach.

THE QUALITIES OF A CREATIVE PERSON

- persistent and stubborn
- takes risks
- open to new experiences
- shows interest in paradox and originality
- enthusiastic and energetic
- is able to concentrate and judge.
- challenges and accepts criticism.

TOP TIPS

- **Think creatively every day.** Creativity is a state of mind that you must encourage every day, not just in the office. Your environment can be your greatest source of inspiration, so pay attention to it: in the morning while reading the newspaper, when on the road travelling home from work listening to the radio, at noon while fetching your lunch...all of these are great opportunities to develop your imagination.
- **Fight your inhibitions and free yourself from conventional thought patterns.** Fear of ridicule, being ostracised or failing will hold you back in your search for new ideas. But ask yourself this question: what have you got to lose? Actually, not much. You have everything to gain by showing your creativity, launching yourself out of your conformism. Start by showing this extravagance through your clothes or a daring new hairstyle.
- **Take advantage of your mistakes.** Have you counted on ideas that didn't work? Don't be hard on yourself, failures and errors are part of the creative process. By looking at your discoveries from a new angle a few days later, you might produce the idea of the year.
- **Practice again and again.** You know that creativity is an endless process. Once you have tasted its benefits, keep practicing it. At home, invent games with your children; in the office, make suggestions to your boss; at the supermarket, invent a new recipe, etc. Afterwards, take notes. Seeing your ideas on paper already gives them weight and strengthens your ability to imagine. By rereading them a

few days later, you can proudly say: "I thought of that".

- **Be curious and try new experiences.** There is no better way to see things differently and therefore stimulate your creative mind. Try a new sport, go to see an exhibition of an artist you have never heard of or a lecture on a topic you know nothing about. You might even discover new aspirations.
- **Be patient.** Developing your creativity won't happen overnight. Establish a small ritual to practice every day, during which you will work on your imagination and take time: big ideas are built up gradually.
- **Nurture your inner child.** It is well known that children have vivid imaginations. Take inspiration from them. Put yourself in their shoes and try to see things in a playful way. If you are lucky enough to have children, play with them to understand how they express their creativity.
- **Choose the creative process rather than the result.** The path to developing your creativity is the most important, not the final idea. Whether your thoughts lead to an innovation or concrete project or not is another matter, but you should already be able to produce ideas. Don't put the cart before the horse, just focus on taking the first step.
- **Practice asking "What if…".** These two little words can open many doors. Forget the term "impossible" and look at the options available to you. What if…you could fly? What if…you were the President of the United States? What if…humans had four hands?

FAQS

ARE WE ALL CREATIVE?

We are all undoubtedly creative, even if we do not express this skill in the same way. According to neurobiologists, we are all equipped with a brain capable of creating, changing and adapting. During the creation process, our two cerebral hemispheres play a prominent role, but we also solicit other neutral circuits of the brain that reactivate parts of our emotional memory. Todd Lubart, a psychology researcher and specialist in creativity, has studied this particular mechanism, theorised under the name of "emotional resonance". What is this about? Each concept, experience or piece of knowledge stored in our memories is associated with emotional memories. So, when we think of a concept, the emotion tied to it resurfaces and can also awaken a feeling buried in a neighbouring feeling who, by an associative logic, then activates a new thought. Therefore, according to Todd Lubart, the more we welcome our emotions, the more we will develop our creativity.

IS CREATIVITY A RECOGNISED SKILL IN BUSINESS?

It is clear that creativity is now a key quality in business. A HRD pharmaceutical industry confirms:

> "Creativity is no longer the preserve of researchers from Research & Development, the men of marketing or publicity. This capacity must be expressed at all levels and in all

businesses of the company, without restriction. This is also a criterion taken into consideration when assessing the annual performance of employees." – Anonymous source

To promote the emergence of ideas within companies, the entire organisation must be rethought and redesigned. For example, in many of them, the most creative employees are identified and trained. They then supervise project groups or endorse the function of "I-mentor" (the "I" standing for "innovation"). Needless to say, these increases in responsibility are beneficial when following a career. Furthermore, managerial strategies have also evolved to create a favourable framework for the development of creativity among all employees.

THERE IS ALREADY A CREATIVE HUB IN MY COMPANY; DO I STILL NEED TO DEVELOP MY OWN CREATIVITY?

Of course! While a creative cluster is created in order to find innovative solutions, awakening your creativity can sometimes help you to break a boring routine in your work and in your everyday life. Among other things, you will learn to look at things differently, to challenge and open your field of possibilities. Finally, there is the argument for improving your wellbeing. Therefore, if you do not want to become creative for your business, do it for yourself.

HOW CAN I CONCRETELY DEVELOP A CREATIVE STATE OF MIND?

A few tips can help you:

- Take to the skies once a week. Walled up, constantly confined, you end up losing your sense of perspective. Find a high up place and focus on the horizon. From there, your problems will seem insignificant and your possibilities seem endless.
- Start meetings by playing a guessing game. To lighten the mood and stimulate the participants, ask them about an unusual issue or provide a surprising visual. Nothing works better at activating the neurons.
- Diversify your experiences. The well-oiled rituals of daily life slowly stifle your creativity. Take the initiative to change something every day both in your private life and at the office: improvise new recipes, go for a different dress style, try a new sport, change your schedule at short notice or vary your font character for your emails (while remaining professional, of course).
- Dare to answer with "why not?" rather than "no". Take all suggestions seriously and without prejudice, even those that may seem absurd at first. Who knows? They may prove beneficial later on.
- Imagine the worst to enjoy the best. When you have reviewed all possible disasters, you will find serenity and will persevere in your projects.
- Post inspiring quotes in your office. True nourishment for the mind, they give you something to think about and will boost your creativity, and that of your colleagues.

> "Anyone who has never made a mistake has never tried any-
> thing new." – Albert Einstein (German physicist, 1879-1955)

- Meditate regularly. As proven by numerous artists, re-
  searchers and entrepreneurs, meditation reduces stress
  and stimulates the imagination.

WHAT IS THE DIFFERENCE BETWEEN IMAGINATION, CREATIVITY, INVENTION AND INNOVATION?

We often tend to confuse these terms. Yet, even though they are linked, it is necessary to know the difference:

- Imagination is the "ability of the mind to represent or to form images". It ignores reality and the laws of physics. Therefore, this is a space where anything is possible.
- Creativity is the "ability or power of an individual to create, that is to say, to imagine and create something new". Imagination is a component of creativity, but unlike the first, creativity develops in a particular context, from which it produces new ideas.
- Invention corresponds to the "action of imagining something new". Therefore, it is very close to creativity. However, while creativity remains a stage of thinking, invention brings the new idea into the physical world.
- Innovation describes the act of innovating or the "result of introducing a new thing". It is the firm establishment of a new idea, in order to improve the business.

OVER TO YOU

You now have the key to open the doors to your innovation potential. But do you feel sufficiently confident and equipped to assert your creative talents? Answer these questions, calculate your score and then draw some conclusions.

	Yes	No
I enjoy doing things differently.		
I am passionate about researching solutions.		
Mistakes motivate me.		
I always look for several solutions to a problem.		
Obstacles allow me to push my limits.		
I am always ready to take on new challenges.		
I am emotional, even in the professional environment.		
I appreciate suspense in life, films or books.		
Judgement from other people does not affect me.		
Opposing views help me to develop my ideas.		
I find that I am more creative with others than alone.		
I like having time to let my mind wander.		
I keep my morale up and remain positive in all situations.		
I like to see the development of ideas that I have suggested to others.		
I am not at all afraid of ridicule.		

Results:

- If you answered 'yes' more than 10 times, you have great confidence in your creativity. It seems that you have nurtured your inner child and your imagination. This can be a great asset to you when in difficulty, and can help to turn your failures into opportunities – provided, of course, that you combine your creative talent with a good dose of self-discipline and organisation.
- If you answered 'yes' between 6 and 10 times, your confidence is not consistent. What resistance are you facing? Study your negative responses for better understanding. Are certain circumstances more favourable than others? You may only be able to create with a group, or conversely, only when alone. Simply find out your flaws to fix them.
- If you only answered 'yes' between one and five times, do not worry: you have creative potential, but you simply haven't exercised it. What limiting beliefs are inhibiting you? Knowing that each person has their own ability to create, what could yours be? Accept mistakes and analyse yourself in different contexts to progress. You will eventually be able to overcome your resistance, whether through specific training or personal coaching.

FIND OUT MORE

BIBLIOGRAPHY

* Aznar, G. (2005) *Idées. 100 techniques de créativité*. Paris: Éditions d'Organisation.
* Bellanger, L. (2005) *Libérez votre créativité. De l'imagination à l'innovation gagnante*. Paris: ESF éditeur.
* Bô, D. (2014) Qu'est- ce que l'intelligence creative ? *Marketing études*. [Online]. [Accessed 6 November 2015]. Available from: <http://testconso.typepad.com/marketinge-tudes/2014/02/quest-ce-que-lintelligence-creative-.html>
* Bonnet, V. (2015) *Développer sa créativité*. [Video]. [Accessed 28 October 2015]. Available from: <https://www.youtube.com/watch?v=kUkgvGpufus>
* Cameron, J. (2007) *Libérez votre créativité*. Paris: J'ai Lu.
* Cottraux, J. (2008) *À chacun sa créativité. Einstein, Mozart, Picasso... et nous*. Paris: Odile Jacob.
* De Bono, E. (2005) *Les six chapeaux de la reflexion*. Paris: Eyrolles.
* Duhoux, P. and Jacob, I. (2006) *Développer sa créativité*. Paris: Retz.
* Fardeau, A. (2008). 5 exercices pour développer sa créativité. *Journal du Net*. [Online]. [Accessed 28 October 2015]. Available from: <http://www.journaldunet.com/management/efficacite-personnelle/conseil/5-exercices-pour-stimu-ler-sa-creativite/5-exercices-pour-stimuler-sa-creativite.shtml>

- Lubart, T., Mouchiroud, C., Tordjam, S. and Zenasni, F. (2003) *Psychologie de la créativité*. Paris: Armand Colin.
- Swinners, J-L. and Briet, J-M. (2004) *L'intelligence créative au- delà du brainstorming*. Paris: Maxima.

ADDITIONAL SOURCES

- Berne, E. (2012) *Intuition et États du moi*. Paris: InterÉditions.
- Cauvin, P. (2013) *Décryptez les types de personnalité avec le MBTI*. Paris: ESF éditeur.
- Charlier, M. (2015) *Comment organiser un workshop productif?* Brussels: Lemaitre Publishing.
- Csikszentmihaly, M. (2006) *La créativité. Psychologie de la découverte et de l'invention*. Paris: Robert Laffont.
- De Bono, E. (2008) *Comment avoir des idées créatives?* Paris: Leduc.s.
- Lecomte, M. (2015) *Comment élaborer une mind map?* Brussels: Lemaitre Publishing.
- Osborn, A. (1959) *L'imagination constructive : principes et processus de la pensée créative et du brainstorming*. Paris: Dunod.
- Centre National de Ressources Textuelles et Lexicales (2016) *CNRTL*. [Online]. [Accessed 28 October 2015]. Available from: <http://www.cnrtl.fr/>
- Sternberg, R. (2007) *Manuel de psychologie cognitive. Du laboratoire à la vie quotidienne*. Brussels: De Boeck.
- Zinque, N. (2015) *Comment innover en équipe ? Astuces pour un brainstorming fructueux*. Brussels: Lemaitre Publishing.

Made in the USA
Monee, IL
07 July 2026